Dream Journal

© Copyright 2021 - All rights reserved.

You may not reproduce, duplicate or send the contents of this book without direct written permission from the author. You cannot hereby despite any circumstance blame the publisher or hold him or her to legal responsibility for any reparation, compensations, or monetary forfeiture owing to the information included herein, either in a direct or an indirect way.

Legal Notice: This book has copyright protection. You can use the book for personal purpose. You should not sell, use, alter, distribute, quote, take excerpts or paraphrase in part or whole the material contained in this book without obtaining the permission of the author first.

Disclaimer Notice: You must take note that the information in this document is for casual reading and entertainment purposes only.
We have made every attempt to provide accurate, up to date and reliable information. We do not express or imply guarantees of any kind. The persons who read admit that the writer is not occupied in giving legal, financial, medical or other advice. We put this book content by sourcing various places.

Please consult a licensed professional before you try any techniques shown in this book. By going through this document, the book lover comes to an agreement that under no situation is the author accountable for any forfeiture, direct or indirect, which they may incur because of the use of material contained in this document, including, but not limited to, — errors, omissions, or inaccuracies.

THIS DREAM JOURNAL BELONGS TO

_____

_____

DATE _____

Thoughts Before Sleeping
_____
_____
_____

Emotions Before Sleeping
_____
_____
_____

What Was I Doing?
_____
_____
_____

Who Was I?
_____
_____
_____

Whose With Me?
_____
_____
_____

Where Was I?

_____
_____
_____

How Did I Feel In The Dream?

_____
_____
_____

What Did I See?

_____
_____
_____

What Did I Learned?

_____
_____
_____

Feeling Upon Awakening

_____
_____
_____

Was The Dream…

RECURRING	LUCID	NIGHTMARE
☐ YES ☐ NO	☐ YES ☐ NO	☐ YES ☐ NO

DATE _____

Thoughts Before Sleeping
_____
_____
_____

Emotions Before Sleeping
_____
_____
_____

What Was I Doing?
_____
_____
_____

Who Was I?
_____
_____
_____

Whose With Me?
_____
_____
_____

Where Was I?

_____
_____
_____

How Did I Feel In The Dream?

_____
_____
_____

What Did I See?

_____
_____
_____

What Did I Learned?

_____
_____
_____

Feeling Upon Awakening

_____
_____
_____

Was The Dream…

RECURRING	LUCID	NIGHTMARE
☐ YES ☐ NO	☐ YES ☐ NO	☐ YES ☐ NO

DATE _____

Thoughts Before Sleeping
_____
_____
_____

Emotions Before Sleeping
_____
_____
_____

What Was I Doing?
_____
_____
_____

Who Was I?
_____
_____
_____

Whose With Me?
_____
_____
_____

Where Was I?

_____
_____
_____

How Did I Feel In The Dream?

_____
_____
_____

What Did I See?

_____
_____
_____

What Did I Learned?

_____
_____
_____

Feeling Upon Awakening

_____
_____
_____

Was The Dream…

RECURRING		LUCID		NIGHTMARE	
☐	☐	☐	☐	☐	☐
YES	NO	YES	NO	YES	NO

DATE _____

Thoughts Before Sleeping
_____
_____
_____

Emotions Before Sleeping
_____
_____
_____

What Was I Doing?
_____
_____
_____

Who Was I?
_____
_____
_____

Whose With Me?
_____
_____
_____

Where Was I?

_____
_____
_____

How Did I Feel In The Dream?

_____
_____
_____

What Did I See?

_____
_____
_____

What Did I Learned?

_____
_____
_____

Feeling Upon Awakening

_____
_____
_____

Was The Dream...

RECURRING	LUCID	NIGHTMARE
☐ YES ☐ NO	☐ YES ☐ NO	☐ YES ☐ NO

DATE _____

Thoughts Before Sleeping
_____
_____
_____

Emotions Before Sleeping
_____
_____
_____

What Was I Doing?
_____
_____
_____

Who Was I?
_____
_____
_____

Whose With Me?
_____
_____
_____

Where Was I?

_____
_____
_____

How Did I Feel In The Dream?

_____
_____
_____

What Did I See?

_____
_____
_____

What Did I Learned?

_____
_____
_____

Feeling Upon Awakening

_____
_____
_____

Was The Dream…

RECURRING		LUCID		NIGHTMARE	
☐	☐	☐	☐	☐	☐
YES	NO	YES	NO	YES	NO

DATE _____

Thoughts Before Sleeping

_____
_____
_____

Emotions Before Sleeping

_____
_____
_____

What Was I Doing?

_____
_____
_____

Who Was I?

_____
_____
_____

Whose With Me?

_____
_____
_____

Where Was I?

_____
_____
_____

How Did I Feel In The Dream?

_____
_____
_____

What Did I See?

_____
_____
_____

What Did I Learned?

_____
_____
_____

Feeling Upon Awakening

_____
_____
_____

Was The Dream…

RECURRING	LUCID	NIGHTMARE
☐ YES ☐ NO	☐ YES ☐ NO	☐ YES ☐ NO

DATE _____

Thoughts Before Sleeping
_____
_____
_____

Emotions Before Sleeping
_____
_____
_____

What Was I Doing?
_____
_____
_____

Who Was I?
_____
_____
_____

Whose With Me?
_____
_____
_____

Where Was I?

_____
_____
_____

How Did I Feel In The Dream?

_____
_____
_____

What Did I See?

_____
_____
_____

What Did I Learned?

_____
_____
_____

Feeling Upon Awakening

_____
_____
_____

Was The Dream...

RECURRING	LUCID	NIGHTMARE
☐ YES ☐ NO	☐ YES ☐ NO	☐ YES ☐ NO

DATE _____

Thoughts Before Sleeping
_____
_____
_____

Emotions Before Sleeping
_____
_____
_____

What Was I Doing?
_____
_____
_____

Who Was I?
_____
_____
_____

Whose With Me?
_____
_____
_____

Where Was I?

_____
_____
_____

How Did I Feel In The Dream?

_____
_____
_____

What Did I See?

_____
_____
_____

What Did I Learned?

_____
_____
_____

Feeling Upon Awakening

_____
_____
_____

Was The Dream…

RECURRING	LUCID	NIGHTMARE
☐ YES ☐ NO	☐ YES ☐ NO	☐ YES ☐ NO

DATE _____

Thoughts Before Sleeping
_____
_____
_____

Emotions Before Sleeping
_____
_____
_____

What Was I Doing?
_____
_____
_____

Who Was I?
_____
_____
_____

Whose With Me?
_____
_____
_____

Where Was I?

_____
_____
_____

How Did I Feel In The Dream?

_____
_____
_____

What Did I See?

_____
_____
_____

What Did I Learned?

_____
_____
_____

Feeling Upon Awakening

_____
_____
_____

Was The Dream...

RECURRING	LUCID	NIGHTMARE
☐ YES ☐ NO	☐ YES ☐ NO	☐ YES ☐ NO

DATE _____

Thoughts Before Sleeping
_____
_____
_____

Emotions Before Sleeping
_____
_____
_____

What Was I Doing?
_____
_____
_____

Who Was I?
_____
_____
_____

Whose With Me?
_____
_____
_____

Where Was I?

_____
_____
_____

How Did I Feel In The Dream?

_____
_____
_____

What Did I See?

_____
_____
_____

What Did I Learned?

_____
_____
_____

Feeling Upon Awakening

_____
_____
_____

Was The Dream…

RECURRING	LUCID	NIGHTMARE
☐ YES ☐ NO	☐ YES ☐ NO	☐ YES ☐ NO

DATE _____

Thoughts Before Sleeping
_____
_____
_____

Emotions Before Sleeping
_____
_____
_____

What Was I Doing?
_____
_____
_____

Who Was I?
_____
_____
_____

Whose With Me?
_____
_____
_____

Where Was I?

_____
_____
_____

How Did I Feel In The Dream?

_____
_____
_____

What Did I See?

_____
_____
_____

What Did I Learned?

_____
_____
_____

Feeling Upon Awakening

_____
_____
_____

Was The Dream...

RECURRING		LUCID		NIGHTMARE	
☐	☐	☐	☐	☐	☐
YES	NO	YES	NO	YES	NO

DATE _____

Thoughts Before Sleeping
_____
_____
_____

Emotions Before Sleeping
_____
_____
_____

What Was I Doing?
_____
_____
_____

Who Was I?
_____
_____
_____

Whose With Me?
_____
_____
_____

Where Was I?

_____
_____
_____

How Did I Feel In The Dream?

_____
_____
_____

What Did I See?

_____
_____
_____

What Did I Learned?

_____
_____
_____

Feeling Upon Awakening

_____
_____
_____

Was The Dream...

RECURRING	LUCID	NIGHTMARE
☐ YES ☐ NO	☐ YES ☐ NO	☐ YES ☐ NO

DATE _____

Thoughts Before Sleeping
_____
_____
_____

Emotions Before Sleeping
_____
_____
_____

What Was I Doing?
_____
_____
_____

Who Was I?
_____
_____
_____

Whose With Me?
_____
_____
_____

Where Was I?

_____
_____
_____

How Did I Feel In The Dream?

_____
_____
_____

What Did I See?

_____
_____
_____

What Did I Learned?

_____
_____
_____

Feeling Upon Awakening

_____
_____
_____

Was The Dream…

RECURRING	LUCID	NIGHTMARE
☐ YES ☐ NO	☐ YES ☐ NO	☐ YES ☐ NO

DATE _____

Thoughts Before Sleeping
_____
_____
_____

Emotions Before Sleeping
_____
_____
_____

What Was I Doing?
_____
_____
_____

Who Was I?
_____
_____
_____

Whose With Me?
_____
_____
_____

Where Was I?

_____
_____
_____

How Did I Feel In The Dream?

_____
_____
_____

What Did I See?

_____
_____
_____

What Did I Learned?

_____
_____
_____

Feeling Upon Awakening

_____
_____
_____

Was The Dream…

RECURRING	LUCID	NIGHTMARE
☐ YES ☐ NO	☐ YES ☐ NO	☐ YES ☐ NO

DATE _____

Thoughts Before Sleeping
_____
_____
_____

Emotions Before Sleeping
_____
_____
_____

What Was I Doing?
_____
_____
_____

Who Was I?
_____
_____
_____

Whose With Me?
_____
_____
_____

Where Was I?

_____
_____
_____

How Did I Feel In The Dream?

_____
_____
_____

What Did I See?

_____
_____
_____

What Did I Learned?

_____
_____
_____

Feeling Upon Awakening

_____
_____
_____

Was The Dream...

RECURRING	LUCID	NIGHTMARE
☐ YES ☐ NO	☐ YES ☐ NO	☐ YES ☐ NO

DATE _____

Thoughts Before Sleeping
_____
_____
_____

Emotions Before Sleeping
_____
_____
_____

What Was I Doing?
_____
_____
_____

Who Was I?
_____
_____
_____

Whose With Me?
_____
_____
_____

Where Was I?

_____
_____
_____

How Did I Feel In The Dream?

_____
_____
_____

What Did I See?

_____
_____
_____

What Did I Learned?

_____
_____
_____

Feeling Upon Awakening

_____
_____
_____

Was The Dream…

RECURRING		LUCID		NIGHTMARE	
☐	☐	☐	☐	☐	☐
YES	NO	YES	NO	YES	NO

DATE _____

Thoughts Before Sleeping
_____
_____
_____

Emotions Before Sleeping
_____
_____
_____

What Was I Doing?
_____
_____
_____

Who Was I?
_____
_____
_____

Whose With Me?
_____
_____
_____

Where Was I?

_____
_____
_____

How Did I Feel In The Dream?

_____
_____
_____

What Did I See?

_____
_____
_____

What Did I Learned?

_____
_____
_____

Feeling Upon Awakening

_____
_____
_____

Was The Dream…

RECURRING	LUCID	NIGHTMARE
☐ YES ☐ NO	☐ YES ☐ NO	☐ YES ☐ NO

DATE _____

Thoughts Before Sleeping
_____
_____
_____

Emotions Before Sleeping
_____
_____
_____

What Was I Doing?
_____
_____
_____

Who Was I?
_____
_____
_____

Whose With Me?
_____
_____
_____

Where Was I?

_____
_____
_____

How Did I Feel In The Dream?

_____
_____
_____

What Did I See?

_____
_____
_____

What Did I Learned?

_____
_____
_____

Feeling Upon Awakening

_____
_____
_____

Was The Dream…

RECURRING	LUCID	NIGHTMARE
☐ ☐	☐ ☐	☐ ☐
YES NO	YES NO	YES NO

DATE _____

Thoughts Before Sleeping
_____
_____
_____

Emotions Before Sleeping
_____
_____
_____

What Was I Doing?
_____
_____
_____

Who Was I?
_____
_____
_____

Whose With Me?
_____
_____
_____

Where Was I?

_____
_____
_____

How Did I Feel In The Dream?

_____
_____
_____

What Did I See?

_____
_____
_____

What Did I Learned?

_____
_____
_____

Feeling Upon Awakening

_____
_____
_____

Was The Dream…

RECURRING	LUCID	NIGHTMARE
☐ YES ☐ NO	☐ YES ☐ NO	☐ YES ☐ NO

DATE _____

Thoughts Before Sleeping
_____
_____
_____

Emotions Before Sleeping
_____
_____
_____

What Was I Doing?
_____
_____
_____

Who Was I?
_____
_____
_____

Whose With Me?
_____
_____
_____

Where Was I?

_____
_____
_____

How Did I Feel In The Dream?

_____
_____
_____

What Did I See?

_____
_____
_____

What Did I Learned?

_____
_____
_____

Feeling Upon Awakening

_____
_____
_____

Was The Dream…

RECURRING	LUCID	NIGHTMARE
☐ YES ☐ NO	☐ YES ☐ NO	☐ YES ☐ NO

DATE _____

Thoughts Before Sleeping
_____
_____
_____

Emotions Before Sleeping
_____
_____
_____

What Was I Doing?
_____
_____
_____

Who Was I?
_____
_____
_____

Whose With Me?
_____
_____
_____

Where Was I?

_____
_____
_____

How Did I Feel In The Dream?

_____
_____
_____

What Did I See?

_____
_____
_____

What Did I Learned?

_____
_____
_____

Feeling Upon Awakening

_____
_____
_____

Was The Dream...

RECURRING		LUCID		NIGHTMARE	
☐	☐	☐	☐	☐	☐
YES	NO	YES	NO	YES	NO

DATE _____

Thoughts Before Sleeping
_____
_____
_____

Emotions Before Sleeping
_____
_____
_____

What Was I Doing?
_____
_____
_____

Who Was I?
_____
_____
_____

Whose With Me?
_____
_____
_____

Where Was I?

_____
_____
_____

How Did I Feel In The Dream?

_____
_____
_____

What Did I See?

_____
_____
_____

What Did I Learned?

_____
_____
_____

Feeling Upon Awakening

_____
_____
_____

Was The Dream...

RECURRING	LUCID	NIGHTMARE
☐ YES ☐ NO	☐ YES ☐ NO	☐ YES ☐ NO

DATE _____

Thoughts Before Sleeping
_____
_____
_____

Emotions Before Sleeping
_____
_____
_____

What Was I Doing?
_____
_____
_____

Who Was I?
_____
_____
_____

Whose With Me?
_____
_____
_____

Where Was I?

_____
_____
_____

How Did I Feel In The Dream?

_____
_____
_____

What Did I See?

_____
_____
_____

What Did I Learned?

_____
_____
_____

Feeling Upon Awakening

_____
_____
_____

Was The Dream…

RECURRING	LUCID	NIGHTMARE
☐ YES ☐ NO	☐ YES ☐ NO	☐ YES ☐ NO

DATE _____

Thoughts Before Sleeping
_____
_____
_____

Emotions Before Sleeping
_____
_____
_____

What Was I Doing?
_____
_____
_____

Who Was I?
_____
_____
_____

Whose With Me?
_____
_____
_____

Where Was I?
_____
_____
_____

How Did I Feel In The Dream?
_____
_____
_____

What Did I See?
_____
_____
_____

What Did I Learned?
_____
_____
_____

Feeling Upon Awakening
_____
_____
_____

Was The Dream...

RECURRING	LUCID	NIGHTMARE
☐ YES ☐ NO	☐ YES ☐ NO	☐ YES ☐ NO

DATE _____

Thoughts Before Sleeping
_____
_____
_____

Emotions Before Sleeping
_____
_____
_____

What Was I Doing?
_____
_____
_____

Who Was I?
_____
_____
_____

Whose With Me?
_____
_____
_____

Where Was I?

_____
_____
_____

How Did I Feel In The Dream?

_____
_____
_____

What Did I See?

_____
_____
_____

What Did I Learned?

_____
_____
_____

Feeling Upon Awakening

_____
_____
_____

Was The Dream...

RECURRING	LUCID	NIGHTMARE
☐ YES ☐ NO	☐ YES ☐ NO	☐ YES ☐ NO

DATE _____

Thoughts Before Sleeping
_____
_____
_____

Emotions Before Sleeping
_____
_____
_____

What Was I Doing?
_____
_____
_____

Who Was I?
_____
_____
_____

Whose With Me?
_____
_____
_____

Where Was I?

_____
_____
_____

How Did I Feel In The Dream?

_____
_____
_____

What Did I See?

_____
_____
_____

What Did I Learned?

_____
_____
_____

Feeling Upon Awakening

_____
_____
_____

Was The Dream…

RECURRING	LUCID	NIGHTMARE
☐ YES ☐ NO	☐ YES ☐ NO	☐ YES ☐ NO

DATE _____

Thoughts Before Sleeping
_____
_____
_____

Emotions Before Sleeping
_____
_____
_____

What Was I Doing?
_____
_____
_____

Who Was I?
_____
_____
_____

Whose With Me?
_____
_____
_____

Where Was I?

_____
_____
_____

How Did I Feel In The Dream?

_____
_____
_____

What Did I See?

_____
_____
_____

What Did I Learned?

_____
_____
_____

Feeling Upon Awakening

_____
_____
_____

Was The Dream…

RECURRING	LUCID	NIGHTMARE
☐ YES ☐ NO	☐ YES ☐ NO	☐ YES ☐ NO

DATE _____

Thoughts Before Sleeping
_____
_____
_____

Emotions Before Sleeping
_____
_____
_____

What Was I Doing?
_____
_____
_____

Who Was I?
_____
_____
_____

Whose With Me?
_____
_____
_____

Where Was I?

_____
_____
_____

How Did I Feel In The Dream?

_____
_____
_____

What Did I See?

_____
_____
_____

What Did I Learned?

_____
_____
_____

Feeling Upon Awakening

_____
_____
_____

Was The Dream…

RECURRING		LUCID		NIGHTMARE	
☐	☐	☐	☐	☐	☐
YES	NO	YES	NO	YES	NO

DATE _____

Thoughts Before Sleeping
_____
_____
_____

Emotions Before Sleeping
_____
_____
_____

What Was I Doing?
_____
_____
_____

Who Was I?
_____
_____
_____

Whose With Me?
_____
_____
_____

Where Was I?

_____
_____
_____

How Did I Feel In The Dream?

_____
_____
_____

What Did I See?

_____
_____
_____

What Did I Learned?

_____
_____
_____

Feeling Upon Awakening

_____
_____
_____

Was The Dream…

RECURRING	LUCID	NIGHTMARE
☐ YES ☐ NO	☐ YES ☐ NO	☐ YES ☐ NO

DATE _____

Thoughts Before Sleeping
_____
_____
_____

Emotions Before Sleeping
_____
_____
_____

What Was I Doing?
_____
_____
_____

Who Was I?
_____
_____
_____

Whose With Me?
_____
_____
_____

Where Was I?

_____
_____
_____

How Did I Feel In The Dream?

_____
_____
_____

What Did I See?

_____
_____
_____

What Did I Learned?

_____
_____
_____

Feeling Upon Awakening

_____
_____
_____

Was The Dream…

RECURRING	LUCID	NIGHTMARE
☐ YES ☐ NO	☐ YES ☐ NO	☐ YES ☐ NO

DATE _____

Thoughts Before Sleeping
_____
_____
_____

Emotions Before Sleeping
_____
_____
_____

What Was I Doing?
_____
_____
_____

Who Was I?
_____
_____
_____

Whose With Me?
_____
_____
_____

Where Was I?

_____
_____
_____

How Did I Feel In The Dream?

_____
_____
_____

What Did I See?

_____
_____
_____

What Did I Learned?

_____
_____
_____

Feeling Upon Awakening

_____
_____
_____

Was The Dream…

RECURRING	LUCID	NIGHTMARE
☐ YES ☐ NO	☐ YES ☐ NO	☐ YES ☐ NO

DATE _____

Thoughts Before Sleeping

_____
_____
_____

Emotions Before Sleeping

_____
_____
_____

What Was I Doing?

_____
_____
_____

Who Was I?

_____
_____
_____

Whose With Me?

_____
_____
_____

Where Was I?

_____
_____
_____

How Did I Feel In The Dream?

_____
_____
_____

What Did I See?

_____
_____
_____

What Did I Learned?

_____
_____
_____

Feeling Upon Awakening

_____
_____
_____

Was The Dream…

RECURRING	LUCID	NIGHTMARE
☐ YES ☐ NO	☐ YES ☐ NO	☐ YES ☐ NO

DATE _____

Thoughts Before Sleeping
_____
_____
_____

Emotions Before Sleeping
_____
_____
_____

What Was I Doing?
_____
_____
_____

Who Was I?
_____
_____
_____

Whose With Me?
_____
_____
_____

Where Was I?

_____
_____
_____

How Did I Feel In The Dream?

_____
_____
_____

What Did I See?

_____
_____
_____

What Did I Learned?

_____
_____
_____

Feeling Upon Awakening

_____
_____
_____

Was The Dream...

RECURRING	LUCID	NIGHTMARE
☐ YES ☐ NO	☐ YES ☐ NO	☐ YES ☐ NO

DATE _____

Thoughts Before Sleeping
_____
_____
_____

Emotions Before Sleeping
_____
_____
_____

What Was I Doing?
_____
_____
_____

Who Was I?
_____
_____
_____

Whose With Me?
_____
_____
_____

Where Was I?

_____
_____
_____

How Did I Feel In The Dream?

_____
_____
_____

What Did I See?

_____
_____
_____

What Did I Learned?

_____
_____
_____

Feeling Upon Awakening

_____
_____
_____

Was The Dream...

RECURRING	LUCID	NIGHTMARE
☐ YES ☐ NO	☐ YES ☐ NO	☐ YES ☐ NO

DATE _____

Thoughts Before Sleeping
_____
_____
_____

Emotions Before Sleeping
_____
_____
_____

What Was I Doing?
_____
_____
_____

Who Was I?
_____
_____
_____

Whose With Me?
_____
_____
_____

Where Was I?

_____
_____
_____

How Did I Feel In The Dream?

_____
_____
_____

What Did I See?

_____
_____
_____

What Did I Learned?

_____
_____
_____

Feeling Upon Awakening

_____
_____
_____

Was The Dream...

RECURRING	LUCID	NIGHTMARE
☐ YES ☐ NO	☐ YES ☐ NO	☐ YES ☐ NO

DATE _____

Thoughts Before Sleeping
_____
_____
_____

Emotions Before Sleeping
_____
_____
_____

What Was I Doing?
_____
_____
_____

Who Was I?
_____
_____
_____

Whose With Me?
_____
_____
_____

Where Was I?

_____
_____
_____

How Did I Feel In The Dream?

_____
_____
_____

What Did I See?

_____
_____
_____

What Did I Learned?

_____
_____
_____

Feeling Upon Awakening

_____
_____
_____

Was The Dream…

RECURRING	LUCID	NIGHTMARE
☐ YES ☐ NO	☐ YES ☐ NO	☐ YES ☐ NO

DATE _____

Thoughts Before Sleeping
_____
_____
_____

Emotions Before Sleeping
_____
_____
_____

What Was I Doing?
_____
_____
_____

Who Was I?
_____
_____
_____

Whose With Me?
_____
_____
_____

Where Was I?

_____
_____
_____

How Did I Feel In The Dream?

_____
_____
_____

What Did I See?

_____
_____
_____

What Did I Learned?

_____
_____
_____

Feeling Upon Awakening

_____
_____
_____

Was The Dream…

RECURRING		LUCID		NIGHTMARE	
☐	☐	☐	☐	☐	☐
YES	NO	YES	NO	YES	NO

DATE _____

Thoughts Before Sleeping
_____
_____
_____

Emotions Before Sleeping
_____
_____
_____

What Was I Doing?
_____
_____
_____

Who Was I?
_____
_____
_____

Whose With Me?
_____
_____
_____

Where Was I?

_____
_____
_____

How Did I Feel In The Dream?

_____
_____
_____

What Did I See?

_____
_____
_____

What Did I Learned?

_____
_____
_____

Feeling Upon Awakening

_____
_____
_____

Was The Dream…

RECURRING	LUCID	NIGHTMARE
☐ YES ☐ NO	☐ YES ☐ NO	☐ YES ☐ NO

DATE _____

Thoughts Before Sleeping
_____
_____
_____

Emotions Before Sleeping
_____
_____
_____

What Was I Doing?
_____
_____
_____

Who Was I?
_____
_____
_____

Whose With Me?
_____
_____
_____

Where Was I?

_____

_____

_____

How Did I Feel In The Dream?

_____

_____

_____

What Did I See?

_____

_____

_____

What Did I Learned?

_____

_____

_____

Feeling Upon Awakening

_____

_____

_____

Was The Dream…

RECURRING	LUCID	NIGHTMARE
☐ ☐	☐ ☐	☐ ☐
YES NO	YES NO	YES NO

DATE _____

Thoughts Before Sleeping

_____
_____
_____

Emotions Before Sleeping

_____
_____
_____

What Was I Doing?

_____
_____
_____

Who Was I?

_____
_____
_____

Whose With Me?

_____
_____
_____

Where Was I?

_____
_____
_____

How Did I Feel In The Dream?

_____
_____
_____

What Did I See?

_____
_____
_____

What Did I Learned?

_____
_____
_____

Feeling Upon Awakening

_____
_____
_____

Was The Dream…

RECURRING	LUCID	NIGHTMARE
☐ YES ☐ NO	☐ YES ☐ NO	☐ YES ☐ NO

DATE _____

Thoughts Before Sleeping
_____
_____
_____

Emotions Before Sleeping
_____
_____
_____

What Was I Doing?
_____
_____
_____

Who Was I?
_____
_____
_____

Whose With Me?
_____
_____
_____

Where Was I?

_____
_____
_____

How Did I Feel In The Dream?

_____
_____
_____

What Did I See?

_____
_____
_____

What Did I Learned?

_____
_____
_____

Feeling Upon Awakening

_____
_____
_____

Was The Dream…

RECURRING		LUCID		NIGHTMARE	
☐	☐	☐	☐	☐	☐
YES	NO	YES	NO	YES	NO

DATE _____

Thoughts Before Sleeping
_____
_____
_____

Emotions Before Sleeping
_____
_____
_____

What Was I Doing?
_____
_____
_____

Who Was I?
_____
_____
_____

Whose With Me?
_____
_____
_____

Where Was I?

_____
_____
_____

How Did I Feel In The Dream?

_____
_____
_____

What Did I See?

_____
_____
_____

What Did I Learned?

_____
_____
_____

Feeling Upon Awakening

_____
_____
_____

Was The Dream…

RECURRING	LUCID	NIGHTMARE
☐ YES ☐ NO	☐ YES ☐ NO	☐ YES ☐ NO

DATE _____

Thoughts Before Sleeping
_____
_____
_____

Emotions Before Sleeping
_____
_____
_____

What Was I Doing?
_____
_____
_____

Who Was I?
_____
_____
_____

Whose With Me?
_____
_____
_____

Where Was I?

_____
_____
_____

How Did I Feel In The Dream?

_____
_____
_____

What Did I See?

_____
_____
_____

What Did I Learned?

_____
_____
_____

Feeling Upon Awakening

_____
_____
_____

Was The Dream…

RECURRING	LUCID	NIGHTMARE
☐ YES ☐ NO	☐ YES ☐ NO	☐ YES ☐ NO

DATE _____

Thoughts Before Sleeping
_____
_____
_____

Emotions Before Sleeping
_____
_____
_____

What Was I Doing?
_____
_____
_____

Who Was I?
_____
_____
_____

Whose With Me?
_____
_____
_____

Where Was I?

_____
_____
_____

How Did I Feel In The Dream?

_____
_____
_____

What Did I See?

_____
_____
_____

What Did I Learned?

_____
_____
_____

Feeling Upon Awakening

_____
_____
_____

Was The Dream…

RECURRING	LUCID	NIGHTMARE
☐ YES ☐ NO	☐ YES ☐ NO	☐ YES ☐ NO

DATE _____

Thoughts Before Sleeping
_____
_____
_____

Emotions Before Sleeping
_____
_____
_____

What Was I Doing?
_____
_____
_____

Who Was I?
_____
_____
_____

Whose With Me?
_____
_____
_____

Where Was I?

_____
_____
_____

How Did I Feel In The Dream?

_____
_____
_____

What Did I See?

_____
_____
_____

What Did I Learned?

_____
_____
_____

Feeling Upon Awakening

_____
_____
_____

Was The Dream…

RECURRING	LUCID	NIGHTMARE
☐ ☐	☐ ☐	☐ ☐
YES NO	YES NO	YES NO

DATE _____

Thoughts Before Sleeping
_____
_____
_____

Emotions Before Sleeping
_____
_____
_____

What Was I Doing?
_____
_____
_____

Who Was I?
_____
_____
_____

Whose With Me?
_____
_____
_____

Where Was I?

_____
_____
_____

How Did I Feel In The Dream?

_____
_____
_____

What Did I See?

_____
_____
_____

What Did I Learned?

_____
_____
_____

Feeling Upon Awakening

_____
_____
_____

Was The Dream…

RECURRING	LUCID	NIGHTMARE
☐ YES ☐ NO	☐ YES ☐ NO	☐ YES ☐ NO

DATE _____

Thoughts Before Sleeping
_____
_____
_____

Emotions Before Sleeping
_____
_____
_____

What Was I Doing?
_____
_____
_____

Who Was I?
_____
_____
_____

Whose With Me?
_____
_____
_____

Where Was I?

_____
_____
_____

How Did I Feel In The Dream?

_____
_____
_____

What Did I See?

_____
_____
_____

What Did I Learned?

_____
_____
_____

Feeling Upon Awakening

_____
_____
_____

Was The Dream…

RECURRING	LUCID	NIGHTMARE
☐ YES ☐ NO	☐ YES ☐ NO	☐ YES ☐ NO

DATE _____

Thoughts Before Sleeping
_____
_____
_____

Emotions Before Sleeping
_____
_____
_____

What Was I Doing?
_____
_____
_____

Who Was I?
_____
_____
_____

Whose With Me?
_____
_____
_____

Where Was I?

_____
_____
_____

How Did I Feel In The Dream?

_____
_____
_____

What Did I See?

_____
_____
_____

What Did I Learned?

_____
_____
_____

Feeling Upon Awakening

_____
_____
_____

Was The Dream…

RECURRING	LUCID	NIGHTMARE
☐ YES ☐ NO	☐ YES ☐ NO	☐ YES ☐ NO

DATE _____

Thoughts Before Sleeping
_____
_____
_____

Emotions Before Sleeping
_____
_____
_____

What Was I Doing?
_____
_____
_____

Who Was I?
_____
_____
_____

Whose With Me?
_____
_____
_____

Where Was I?

_____
_____
_____

How Did I Feel In The Dream?

_____
_____
_____

What Did I See?

_____
_____
_____

What Did I Learned?

_____
_____
_____

Feeling Upon Awakening

_____
_____
_____

Was The Dream…

RECURRING	LUCID	NIGHTMARE
☐ YES ☐ NO	☐ YES ☐ NO	☐ YES ☐ NO

DATE _____

Thoughts Before Sleeping
_____
_____
_____

Emotions Before Sleeping
_____
_____
_____

What Was I Doing?
_____
_____
_____

Who Was I?
_____
_____
_____

Whose With Me?
_____
_____
_____

Where Was I?

_____
_____
_____

How Did I Feel In The Dream?

_____
_____
_____

What Did I See?

_____
_____
_____

What Did I Learned?

_____
_____
_____

Feeling Upon Awakening

_____
_____
_____

Was The Dream…

RECURRING	LUCID	NIGHTMARE
☐ YES ☐ NO	☐ YES ☐ NO	☐ YES ☐ NO

DATE _____

Thoughts Before Sleeping

_____
_____
_____

Emotions Before Sleeping

_____
_____
_____

What Was I Doing?

_____
_____
_____

Who Was I?

_____
_____
_____

Whose With Me?

_____
_____
_____

Where Was I?

_____
_____
_____

How Did I Feel In The Dream?

_____
_____
_____

What Did I See?

_____
_____
_____

What Did I Learned?

_____
_____
_____

Feeling Upon Awakening

_____
_____
_____

Was The Dream…

RECURRING		LUCID		NIGHTMARE	
☐	☐	☐	☐	☐	☐
YES	NO	YES	NO	YES	NO

DATE _____

Thoughts Before Sleeping
_____
_____
_____

Emotions Before Sleeping
_____
_____
_____

What Was I Doing?
_____
_____
_____

Who Was I?
_____
_____
_____

Whose With Me?
_____
_____
_____

Where Was I?

_____
_____
_____

How Did I Feel In The Dream?

_____
_____
_____

What Did I See?

_____
_____
_____

What Did I Learned?

_____
_____
_____

Feeling Upon Awakening

_____
_____
_____

Was The Dream...

RECURRING	LUCID	NIGHTMARE
☐ YES ☐ NO	☐ YES ☐ NO	☐ YES ☐ NO

DATE _____

Thoughts Before Sleeping
_____
_____
_____

Emotions Before Sleeping
_____
_____
_____

What Was I Doing?
_____
_____
_____

Who Was I?
_____
_____
_____

Whose With Me?
_____
_____
_____

Where Was I?

_____
_____
_____

How Did I Feel In The Dream?

_____
_____
_____

What Did I See?

_____
_____
_____

What Did I Learned?

_____
_____
_____

Feeling Upon Awakening

_____
_____
_____

Was The Dream…

RECURRING	LUCID	NIGHTMARE
☐ YES ☐ NO	☐ YES ☐ NO	☐ YES ☐ NO

DATE _____

Thoughts Before Sleeping
_____
_____
_____

Emotions Before Sleeping
_____
_____
_____

What Was I Doing?
_____
_____
_____

Who Was I?
_____
_____
_____

Whose With Me?
_____
_____
_____

Where Was I?

_____
_____
_____

How Did I Feel In The Dream?

_____
_____
_____

What Did I See?

_____
_____
_____

What Did I Learned?

_____
_____
_____

Feeling Upon Awakening

_____
_____
_____

Was The Dream...

RECURRING	LUCID	NIGHTMARE
☐ YES ☐ NO	☐ YES ☐ NO	☐ YES ☐ NO

DATE _____

Thoughts Before Sleeping
_____
_____
_____

Emotions Before Sleeping
_____
_____
_____

What Was I Doing?
_____
_____
_____

Who Was I?
_____
_____
_____

Whose With Me?
_____
_____
_____

Where Was I?

_____
_____
_____

How Did I Feel In The Dream?

_____
_____
_____

What Did I See?

_____
_____
_____

What Did I Learned?

_____
_____
_____

Feeling Upon Awakening

_____
_____
_____

Was The Dream...

RECURRING	LUCID	NIGHTMARE
☐ YES ☐ NO	☐ YES ☐ NO	☐ YES ☐ NO

DATE _____

Thoughts Before Sleeping
_____
_____
_____

Emotions Before Sleeping
_____
_____
_____

What Was I Doing?
_____
_____
_____

Who Was I?
_____
_____
_____

Whose With Me?
_____
_____
_____

Where Was I?

_____
_____
_____

How Did I Feel In The Dream?

_____
_____
_____

What Did I See?

_____
_____
_____

What Did I Learned?

_____
_____
_____

Feeling Upon Awakening

_____
_____
_____

Was The Dream…

RECURRING	LUCID	NIGHTMARE
☐ YES ☐ NO	☐ YES ☐ NO	☐ YES ☐ NO

DATE _____

Thoughts Before Sleeping
_____
_____
_____

Emotions Before Sleeping
_____
_____
_____

What Was I Doing?
_____
_____
_____

Who Was I?
_____
_____
_____

Whose With Me?
_____
_____
_____

Where Was I?

_____
_____
_____

How Did I Feel In The Dream?

_____
_____
_____

What Did I See?

_____
_____
_____

What Did I Learned?

_____
_____
_____

Feeling Upon Awakening

_____
_____
_____

Was The Dream…

RECURRING	LUCID	NIGHTMARE
☐ YES ☐ NO	☐ YES ☐ NO	☐ YES ☐ NO

DATE _____

Thoughts Before Sleeping
_____
_____
_____

Emotions Before Sleeping
_____
_____
_____

What Was I Doing?
_____
_____
_____

Who Was I?
_____
_____
_____

Whose With Me?
_____
_____
_____

Where Was I?

_____
_____
_____

How Did I Feel In The Dream?

_____
_____
_____

What Did I See?

_____
_____
_____

What Did I Learned?

_____
_____
_____

Feeling Upon Awakening

_____
_____
_____

Was The Dream...

RECURRING	LUCID	NIGHTMARE
☐ YES ☐ NO	☐ YES ☐ NO	☐ YES ☐ NO

DATE _____

Thoughts Before Sleeping
_____
_____
_____

Emotions Before Sleeping
_____
_____
_____

What Was I Doing?
_____
_____
_____

Who Was I?
_____
_____
_____

Whose With Me?
_____
_____
_____

Where Was I?

_____
_____
_____

How Did I Feel In The Dream?

_____
_____
_____

What Did I See?

_____
_____
_____

What Did I Learned?

_____
_____
_____

Feeling Upon Awakening

_____
_____
_____

Was The Dream…

RECURRING	LUCID	NIGHTMARE
☐ YES ☐ NO	☐ YES ☐ NO	☐ YES ☐ NO

Hey there!!!

We hope you enjoyed our book. As a small family company, your feedback is very important to us. Please let us know how you like our book at:

believepublisher@gmail.com

Without your voice we don't exist!

Please, support us and leave a review!

Thank you!!!

www.ingramcontent.com/pod-product-compliance
Lightning Source LLC
LaVergne TN
LVHW011956070526
838202LV00054B/4932